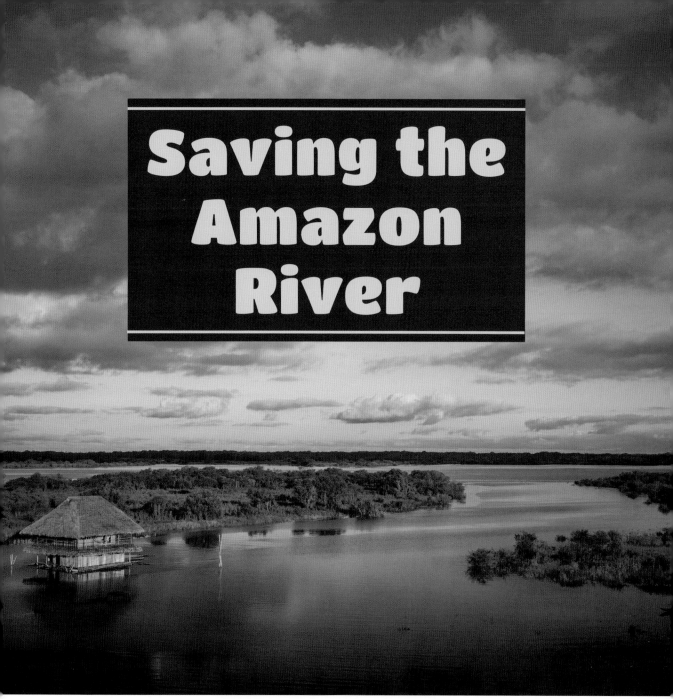

Saving the Amazon River

Written by Anna Porter

Series Consultant: Linda Hoyt

WorldWise™
Content-based Learning

Contents

Chapter 1   Worth saving: Very special spaces on Earth   4

            Significant biosphere reserves   6

Chapter 2   The Amazon River Basin   8

            Why is the Amazon River important?   8

            The climate of the Amazon   10

            Why is the Amazon Rainforest important?   12

            Why do animals need the rainforest?   14

Chapter 3   Biosphere reserves in the Amazon   16

            How is the health of biosphere
            reserves maintained?   18

Chapter 4   What are the threats to the Amazon River Basin?   20

            Forest clearing   20

            Changing climate   22

            Polluting industries   24

            How is the atmosphere being damaged?   25

            Smog and acid rain   26

Chapter 5   Who is helping to save the Amazon?   28

Conclusion   30

Glossary   31

Index   32

Chapter 1

Worth saving: Very special places on Earth

There are many regions on Earth that scientists agree should be listed as special environmental spaces. They are called protected **biosphere** reserves.

Biosphere reserves are natural habitats for a large diversity of living things or seriously endangered animals or plants. Some are in frozen fragile places, others in hot tropical places. They have landforms or features that exist nowhere else. They are places where scientists can conduct research into the nature of the earth's rocks, its natural resources, its climate, and evidence of changes to it.

Mangroves in a biosphere reserve in the Caribbean Sea

Caucasian biosphere reserve, Russia

In 1970, the United Nations Educational, Scientific and Cultural Organization (UNESCO) established the Man and Biosphere program. It identifies and protects a global network of the planet's major **ecosystems** and their wildlife.

Mirror Lake in a biosphere reserve, China

Flamingos in a biosphere reserve, Mexico

Significant biosphere reserves

Amazon River Basin

Has the largest volume of fresh river water in the world. Its tropical rainforest represents 54% of all remaining rainforest on Earth, and half of all Earth's plants and animals live in it.

Galápagos Islands

Support many endangered **species** found nowhere else on Earth – the giant Galápagos tortoise, Galápagos penguins, marine iguanas and the Galápagos green turtle.

Scientists estimate that more than 30 million different kinds of animals and plants are found in biosphere reserves around the world.

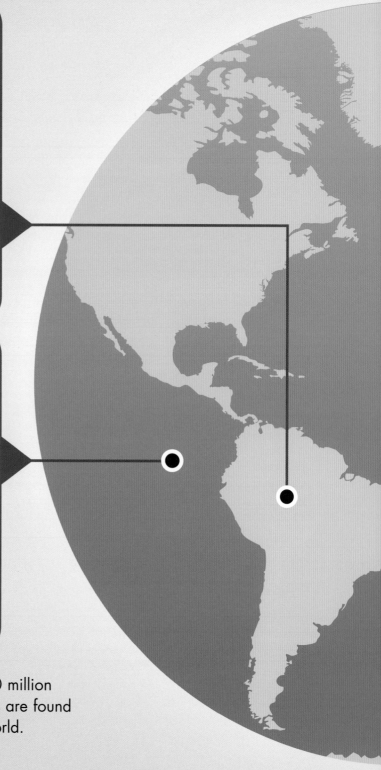

Find out more

Where are some other biosphere reserves? Why do you think they have been listed as worth saving?

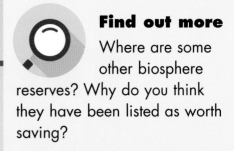

Congo River Basin Reserve

Contains about 32,000 tree species and supports the threatened African forest elephant, the river hog and the endangered sun-tailed monkey.

Antarctica

Contains 90% of all the ice in the world and is the only place in the world where scientists can explore the rocks of Earth's oceanic crust. It provides breeding areas for millions of seabirds and endangered mammals such as southern fur and elephant seals.

Chapter 2

The Amazon River Basin

The Amazon River **Basin** is one of the most significant environments on Earth. It covers an area of about 7 million square kilometres. More than two-thirds of the basin is covered by rainforest. The Amazon River is the greatest river in South America.

Why is the Amazon River important?

Fresh running water on Earth is precious. Nearly all the water on Earth is in the ocean. Most freshwater is in glaciers or underground water systems. Only a tiny fraction is in rivers, streams, lakes and wetlands or in the **atmosphere**. The Amazon River Basin has the largest volume of fresh river water in the world and carries 20 to 25 per cent of all freshwater that runs off the earth's surface.

This river system is of great interest to scientists, who study how it was formed, how it functions today, and the amazing number of plants and animals it supports.

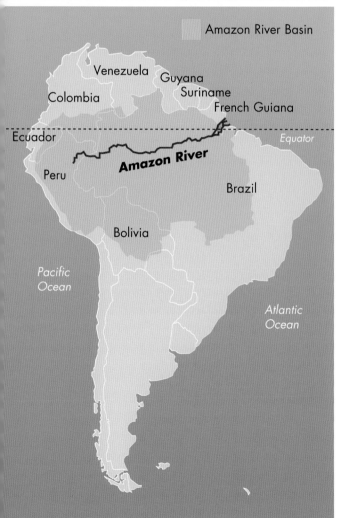

Amazon River Basin

Venezuela
Guyana
Suriname
Colombia
French Guiana
Ecuador
Equator
Amazon River
Peru
Brazil
Bolivia
Pacific
Ocean
Atlantic
Ocean

How long is the Amazon River?

The river is almost 7,000 kilometres long and has 200 smaller river **tributaries** flowing into or from it.

Where does it flow?

The Amazon River begins in the snow-covered Andes Mountains in southern Peru, and flows through several South American countries before reaching the Atlantic Ocean.

What does this river support?

It contains large lakes, swamps and wetlands, and supports the largest tropical rainforest in the world. This rainforest has millions of plants and animals living in it.

The climate of the Amazon

The Amazon River is located on the **equator**. More than one metre of rain falls on the land around the equator each year – over 25 millimetres every day – and most of it runs into the Amazon River.

Tropical rainforests are found in the hot wet climate zone or band near the equator. They are dense and complex ecosystems that have at least 180 centimetres of rainfall with a hot and humid climate. They experience temperatures that hover around 30 degrees Celsius during the day, and stay at about 20 degrees Celsius overnight.

The climate of the Amazon is divided into two main seasons: the wet season and the dry season. In the wet season, the river rises more than nine metres and overflows its banks. In the wettest times, the flooded Amazon Rainforest increases in size by more than three times. In the drier part of the year, when less rain falls, about 108 square kilometres of the Amazon Rainforest are covered in water.

Why is the Amazon Rainforest important?

Much of the heavy rain that falls into the Amazon River and the Amazon Rainforest evaporates and forms a large part of the water vapour in the earth's atmosphere.

Water on the millions of plants in the Amazon River Basin also evaporates and adds to this vapour before it rains. Higher rainfall allows people to grow more food in this region as well as in other countries north of it. This is important in an area of the world where there are lots of people depending on food crops.

The layers in a rainforest support different types of **species** with different needs, and the forest has both wet and drier areas, which mean there are many different ecosystems. These forests contain more living creatures and plants than any other habitat on Earth.

Cocoa pods hanging from tree in the Amazon

Cocoa beans drying

A rosewood tree

Plants are the key to life on Earth because they provide food for other living things. They absorb energy from sunlight and convert it into food.

Trees and plants also release oxygen into the air and improve the condition of the atmosphere. Without this oxygen, few living things can survive. Trees also bind the soil to the ground underneath and stop it from being blown or washed away.

The Amazon River Basin is the largest of its kind in the world and supports millions of species of plants and trees, such as mahogany, cedar, palm and rosewood.

Why do animals need the rainforest?

There are four layers of vegetation in the Amazon Rainforest.
Animals depend on plants in these layers for food and shelter.
The plants depend on these animals to pollinate them or spread
their seeds. Some animals stay in one layer of the rainforest most
of the time; others move between layers to gather food.

Emergent layer

Canopy layer

Understorey layer

Forest floor

Find out more

Find out why flowers in the Amazon Rainforest are important to hummingbirds.

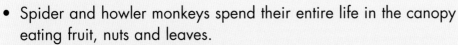

- Harpy eagles nest in these trees but fly down to the lower trees to hunt their prey.
- Groups of capuchin and squirrel monkeys move about and feed on nuts and leaves.
- Morpho butterflies shelter among the tree leaves and gather nectar from flowers for food.

A harpy eagle

- Spider and howler monkeys spend their entire life in the canopy eating fruit, nuts and leaves.
- Sloths spend most of the time here eating leaves and tree fern fronds. They move down once a week to leave droppings on the forest floor.
- Hummingbirds build their nests on branches in this layer.

A sloth

- Large numbers of insects live and feed on the plant life.
- Red-eyed tree frogs move around to eat the insects.
- Jaguars hunt squirrels and birds.

A jaguar

- Many animals eat the ripe fruit and seeds on the ground, or rummage through the leaf litter or bits of bark to eat insects, mice and bats.
- Leaf cutter ants use their strong jaws to cut a leaf into small pieces to take back to their underground nests. The leaf pieces **decay** into a fungus, which they eat.
- Poison dart frogs eat spiders and insects under the leaf litter.

A poison dart frog

Chapter 3

Biosphere reserves in the Amazon

The Amazon River **Basin** contains several interconnected **biosphere** reserves.

Over the years, scientists and **environmentalists** have worked with UNESCO to set aside large areas along the path of the Amazon River as protected reserves.   These reserves form a network to protect the living things within them. Here are four key biosphere reserves.

❶ Peru Pacaya Samiria National Reserve

A giant river otter

Established: 1982
Area: 2 million hectares
Significance:
1,000 wild plants
527 **species** of birds
102 mammal species
69 species of reptiles
269 different kinds of fish

❷ Ecuador Sumaco Biosphere Reserve

Amazon Rainforest, Ecuador

Established: 2000
Area: 206,750 hectares
Significance:
6,000 species of plants
101 species of mammals
86 species of frogs and toads
27 families of fish

❸ Ecuador Yasuni Biosphere Reserve

Amazon landscape, Yasuni

Established: 1989
Area: 1.6 million hectares
Significance:
6,000 species of plants
600 species of birds
204 species of mammals
121 species of reptiles
1,000 species of insects

❹ Brazil Central Amazon Conservation Complex

Giant lily pads float in the Amazon, Brazil.

Established: 2003
Area: 6 million hectares
Significance:
6,000 species of plants
3,000 species of fish
600 species of birds
112 species of reptiles
120 species of mammals
65 species of amphibians

How is the health of biosphere reserves maintained?

Scientists and environmentalists measure the health of a biosphere reserve. They work out how many species of different living things are able to meet their needs in this reserve. This is called maintaining the balance of nature.

People can live within this balance. There are **indigenous** groups of people who need the Amazon Rainforest for food and shelter. They live in a **sustainable** way – hunting, fishing and farming. They choose to live this way, and laws have been passed to respect their right to do so.

Find out more

Find out about other indigenous groups living in the Amazon River Basin.

One indigenous group, the Yanomami, live in houses made of **thatched** vines and leaves. They eat deer, monkeys and armadillo, and grow corn and plantain (a type of banana). But this balance can be easily upset or damaged by natural disasters or by the activities of people.

Chapter 4

What are the threats to the Amazon River Basin?

Forest clearing

When a tree is cut down, other plants in the forest are affected. Each tree or plant provides food and shelter for many animals but they are disappearing at record rates in unprotected areas of the Amazon River **Basin**.

There are increasing numbers of people living on the edge of the river basin who clear the land in the basin to grow food crops and build homes. They cut down forest trees or practise **slash-and-burn** farming techniques. It takes decades for animal and plant numbers to recover. After fires, farmers use the land to grow crops, so many animals and plants lose their forest habitat.

Farming also disturbs the soil. Soil can be blown away more easily, and heavy rainfall washes away nutrients in the soil, so the land becomes less productive and people need to clear forest to get more land for crops. As a result, the size of the Amazon Rainforest is rapidly decreasing.

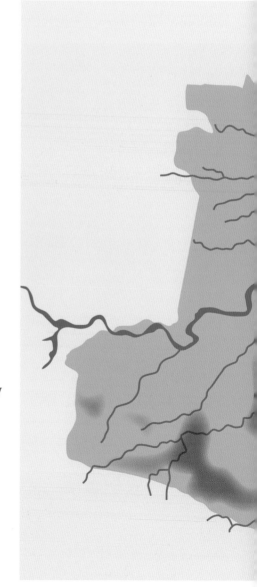

Some farmers use **fertilisers** on their crops, and if these get into rivers and lakes, they cause **algae** to grow much faster. Algae use up the oxygen in the water and cause harm to wildlife.

The more suitable an area is for agriculture, with **arable** land and good water supplies available, the more likely it is to attract humans to live in and around it.

Burning the Amazon Rainforest to clear land for farming

Deforestation in the Amazon River Basin

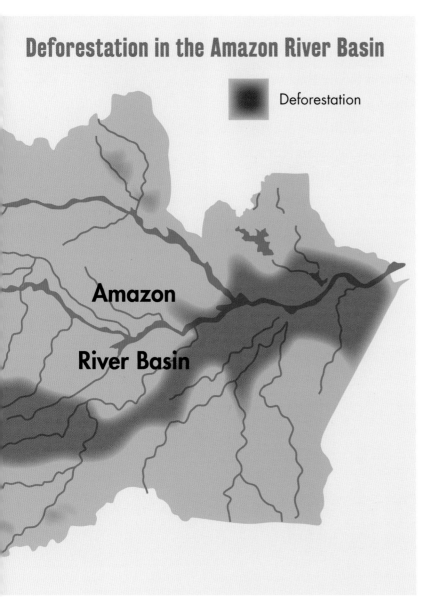

Deforestation

Amazon

River Basin

Clearing land in the Amazon

Rice-growing fields along the Amazon River, Peru

Changing climate

The threat of global warming, as measured by the increasing temperature of the earth and its oceans, affects all **biosphere** reserves and their wildlife. Today's global warming is worrying because it is occurring quickly. Rapid warming could wipe out many **species** in these reserves because they cannot adapt to temperature change and other changing weather patterns. In the Amazon River Basin, the rainforest trees and plants will be affected first, and then the animals that rely on them for food and shelter will suffer.

Rainfall has decreased in the Amazon River Basin because large areas of the rainforest have been cleared for farming and cattle-raising. Drier conditions greatly increase the risk of fire. When fires occur, more carbon dioxide and methane are released into the **atmosphere**, and they increase global warming.

Destroyed rainforest in the Amazon, Brazil

Logs cut from the Amazon Rainforest, Ecuador

Scientists ringing alarm bells!

Scientists say that:

- The average temperature of the planet will be at least 1.5 degrees Celsius higher by the year 2030.
- The sea level has risen about 10.7 centimetres in the past century because of shrinking ice-sheets. This has an effect on the **ecosystems** at the mouth of the Amazon River, which can be flooded and soil washed away.

Cattle farming in the Amazon

Polluting industries

Some industries have polluted the rivers in the Amazon, its forests and nearby oceans. In Brazil, miners extract gold by mixing it with **mercury**. This mercury is often dumped into the rivers. Mercury can kill freshwater wildlife and can poison people if it gets into any water supplies. Gold-mining techniques in the Amazon region of Brazil released more than 3,000 tonnes of mercury between 1987 and 1994.

An oil pipeline leading from a well in the Amazon, Ecuador

Oil in its raw form, known as crude oil, is found below the Yasuni National Park in Ecuador. To extract this oil, several hundred wells have been sunk, and many drilling platforms have been constructed.

Pipes carry the oil over 480 kilometres through the fragile ecosystems in national parks and other protected areas to the Pacific coast and to oil refineries in the United States.

The effects of gold mining in the Amazon

Find out more

Find out how many people now live in the world and what the predicted world population will be by 2100 (the end of this century).

How is the atmosphere being damaged?

The number of people in the world has increased rapidly. Over the past hundred or so years, people have invented or used all sorts of technologies in their daily lives. Some of these have allowed people to fill the atmosphere with harmful gases.

1 The worst polluters are fossil fuels, such as coal, oil and natural gas, that are burned by power stations, cars, buses, trucks, planes and ships.

2 Burning household rubbish emits **toxic** substances.

3 Forest burning not only removes trees, but also allows harmful carbon dioxide to move into the atmosphere.

4 Some products release harmful chemicals into the air when they are used.

25

Smog and acid rain

Smog is caused when gases like sulphur dioxide are released from the exhaust pipes of buses and trucks or from power stations and factories. These gases react with sunlight, rise up high into the atmosphere, dissolve into tiny droplets of moisture and produce a haze or acid rain.

Acid rain can be very harmful to forests as it seeps into the soil and dissolves the existing nutrients that trees need to stay healthy. It weakens trees, causes **dieback** on their leaves and their young shoots die. It also affects the water purity in the rivers of the Amazon and harms wildlife.

Pollution on the Amazon River

Reports of acid rain in Brazil and other parts of the Amazon River Basin indicate that these pollutants are spreading in the atmosphere across the planet. Scientists are now studying the way in which the earth's atmosphere and its biospheres are connected in maintaining a healthy planet.

Chapter 5

Who is helping to save the Amazon?

Laws and regulations protect and manage the Amazon **biosphere** reserves and try to prevent further deforestation. Several organisations have developed plans to conduct and co-ordinate scientific research and education programs. They involve the **indigenous** groups that live in and around the regions. UNESCO oversees these environmental plans in all areas.

The World Wide Fund for Nature (WWF):

- Works with coffee farmers bordering the parks to help them adapt to the unpredictable rainfall and warmer temperatures that are changing the amount of harvest they obtain.

  This will build food security for these farmers and discourage them from clearing more forest for crops. WWF is helping them plant trees, which protect their crops from **erosion** during heavy rain, build new, more efficient irrigation systems and to make use of more organic **fertilisers**.

A coffee crop

- Helps park managers in Peru and Colombia to **reforest** so as to prevent erosion, landslides and pollution of the rivers.

- Establishes freshwater monitoring stations in Ecuador.

- Protects parts of the river habitats in various regions. In Colombia, it is helping to maintain vegetation along rivers, such as the Putumayo, to prevent flooding and erosion, and to moderate the temperature of the river water.

This helps the **migratory** fish, such as catfish and buffalo fish, that provide food to local people. The vegetation provides shelter for animals such as monkeys, which are also food sources.

Putumayo River in the Amazon

Conclusion

Biosphere reserves are listed and protected because they are special environmental spaces on Earth. They contain many significant and endangered **species**, and are sensitive to changes in atmospheric and ocean temperatures and easily damaged by pollution.

Many people, governments and international organisations are therefore working to protect them. Scientists say that now it is up to all of us to take care of them. It is part of our global responsibility. More than ever, people will depend on biosphere reserves like those in the Amazon River **Basin** for cleaner air in our **atmosphere**.

Glossary

algae plant-like living things that can make their own food, mostly found in water

arable good for growing crops

atmosphere the different layers of air that surround Earth

basin the area of land that surrounds a large river and all the smaller rivers and streams that flow into it

biosphere a part of Earth where living things can exist

decay slowly break down

dieback a disease that affects trees and woody plants and causes parts of the plant to die

ecosystems everything in particular environments, including living things, such as plants and animals, and non-living things, such as water and rocks.

environmentalists people who work to protect the natural environment

equator an imaginary line around the Earth that is halfway between the north and south poles

erosion the wearing away of land by wind or water

fertilisers substances (often chemicals) added to the soil to help plants to grow

indigenous the first people to live in a country or area

mercury a metal that is a liquid at regular temperatures

migratory moving from one place to another to find food or look after young in places where the weather is better

reforest planting seeds or young trees in areas where there was once a forest

slash-and-burn cutting down and burning plants to clear land

species a group of living things that are alike in many ways, have many traits in common and are able to have offspring

sustainable can be used without being damaged, destroyed or used up

thatched dried plants used to make roofs

toxic poisonous

Index

acid rain 26–27

Amazon Rainforest 11, 12–15, 17, 18, 20, 21, 23

Amazon River 8, 9, 10, 12, 16, 21, 23, 27

Amazon River Basin 6, 8, 9, 12, 13, 16, 19, 20, 22, 27, 30

Antarctica 7

atmosphere 8, 12, 13, 22, 25, 27, 30

balance of nature 18

biosphere reserves 4, 16–19, 22, 28, 30

climate 10–11, 22–23

Congo River Basin Reserve 7

environmentalists 18

farmers 20, 21, 28

forest clearing 20–21

Galápagos Islands 6

indigenous groups 18

polluting industries 24

scientists 4, 6, 7, 8, 16, 18, 23, 27, 30

slash-and-burn farming 20

smog 26

UNESCO 5, 16, 28

WWF 28

Yanomami 18